THE EUGÉNIE ROCHEROLLE SERIES

Intermediate Piano Solo

Meaningful Moments

8 Piano Solos for Special Occasions by Eugénie Rocherolle

T0081643

With love to my sister,
Barbara Ricau MacArthur

ISBN 978-1-5400-3094-8

HAL•LEONARD®

Visit Hal Leonard Online at
www.halleonard.com

Contact Us:
Hal Leonard
7777 West Bluemound Road
Milwaukee, WI 53213
Email: info@halleonard.com

In Europe contact:
Hal Leonard Europe Limited
Distribution Centre, Newmarket Road
Bury St Edmunds, Suffolk, IP33 3YB
Email: info@halleonardeurope.com

In Australia contact:
Hal Leonard Australia Pty. Ltd.
4 Lentara Court
Cheltenham, Victoria, 3192 Australia
Email: info@halleonard.com.au

FROM THE COMPOSER

Life is comprised of both celebratory and solemn events which almost always require music. It is my hope that this collection will prove to be suitable for any number of occasions and help to bring smiles, or comfort.

ADAGIO was written in memory of a good friend, George Lenz. Because he so admired the music of the great composers, with Bach a particular favorite, I tried to capture the reverence of Bach's music in this tribute.

AMAZING GRACE
Rather than a hymn-like arrangement, this version features key changes and added texture.

AVE MARIA
With the right hand playing the familiar melody as a single line, more attention can be given to the left-hand chord changes and accompaniment patterns.

BRIDAL MARCH was written for my sister, Barbara, whose marriage to Bob MacArthur took place at our parents' home. It was a small wedding, and our youngest sister was maid of honor. After the three-measure introduction, she preceded the bride down the staircase and across the living room to where the exchange of vows took place. I had the pleasure of playing the wedding march on a restored Chickering baby grand player-piano that had originally belonged to my grandmother.

ELEGY was written in memory of Dr. John Metz, professor emeritus, who maintained a private studio where he taught piano and harpsichord. For a number of years he served as president of our area music teachers' association. The original version, scored for piano and cello, was performed *in memoriam* at a Connecticut State Music Teachers Convention in New Haven.

RECESSIONAL can be used for church weddings, graduations, civic occasions, or any event that requires a lengthy exit.

WEDDING MARCH was written for our son, Laurent, and his bride, Holly Appleton. They were married in a small, historic church. The procession of four bridesmaids began after the two-measure introduction. If necessary, the duration of the march can be extended by repeating from measure 3.

WEDDING PROCESSIONAL was written for my own marriage to Didier which took place in a medium-sized church. After the two-measure introduction, the first of the five bridesmaids began the procession down the aisle. If less music is needed, the piece can be played through only once, using the second ending.

Eugénie

Eugénie Rocherolle
June 2018

CONTENTS

ADAGIO

In memory of George F. Lenz

Eugénie Rocherolle

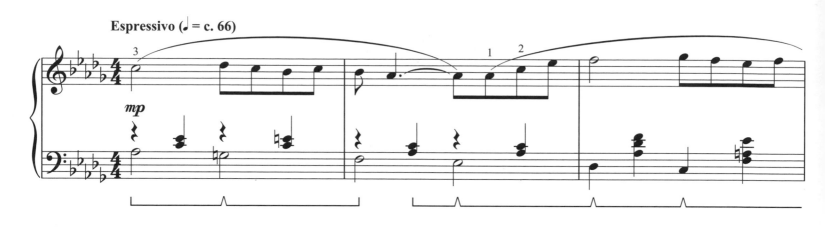

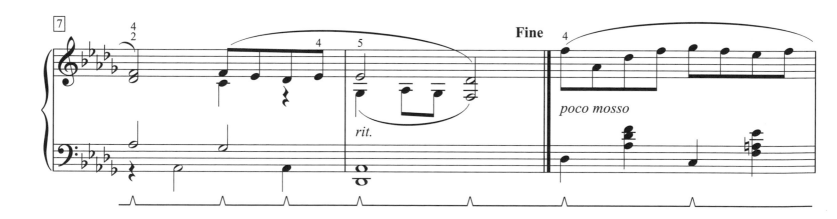

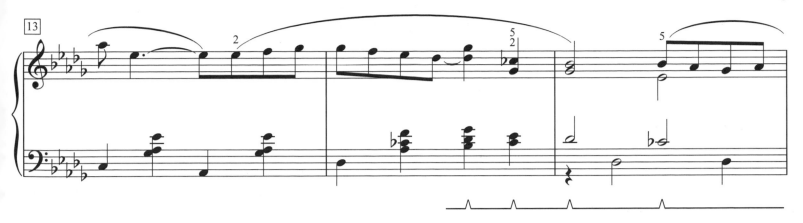

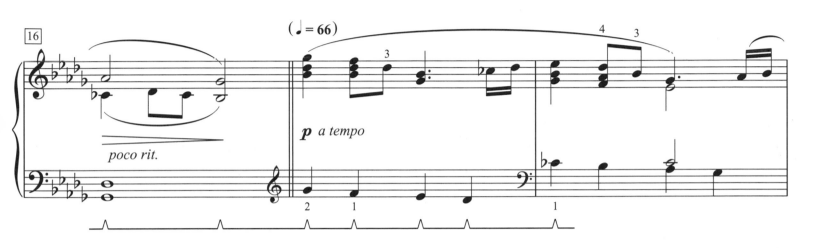

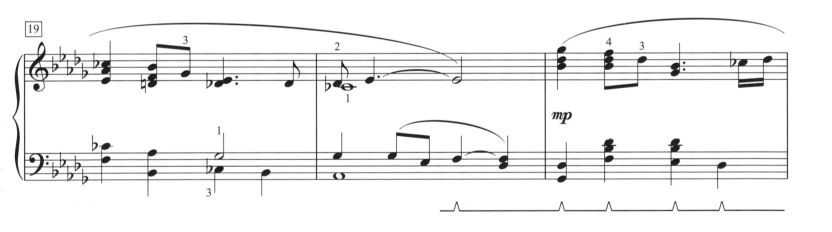

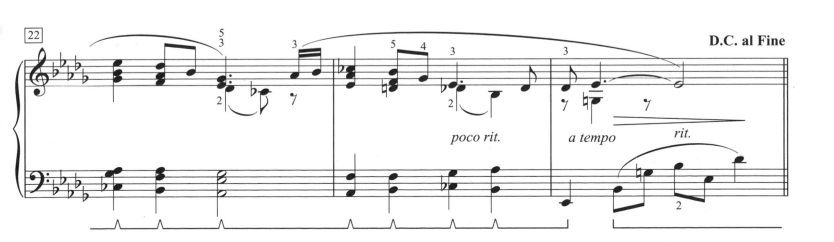

AVE MARIA

FRANZ SCHUBERT
Arranged by EUGÉNIE ROCHEROLLE

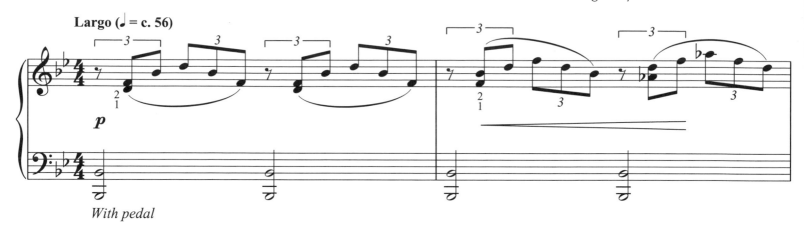

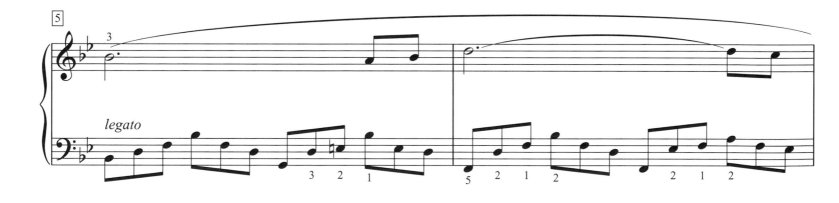

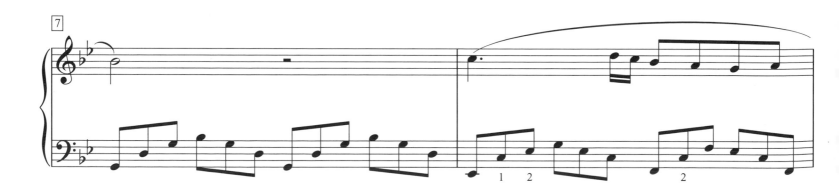

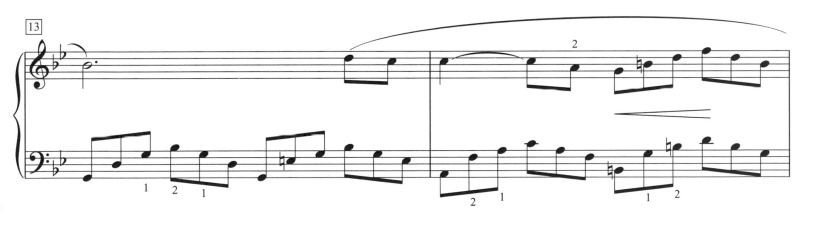

AMAZING GRACE

Traditional
Arranged by EUGÉNIE ROCHEROLLE

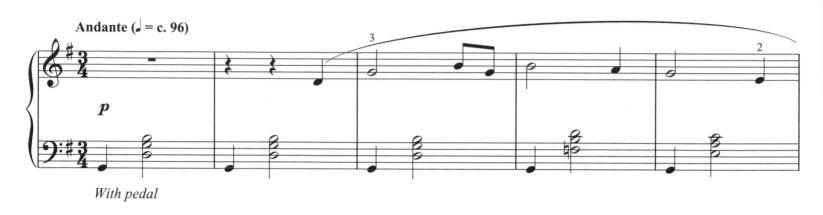

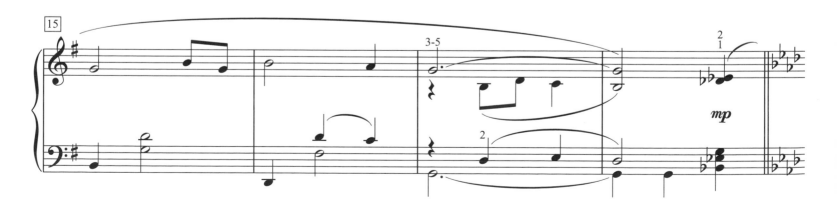

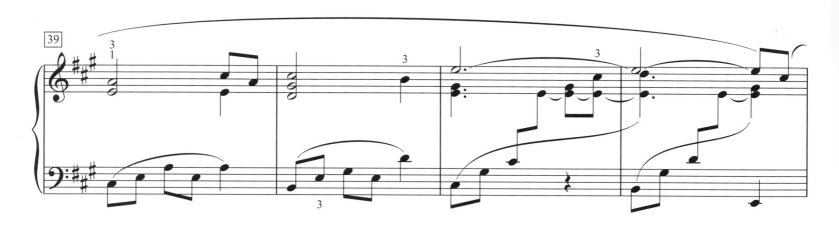

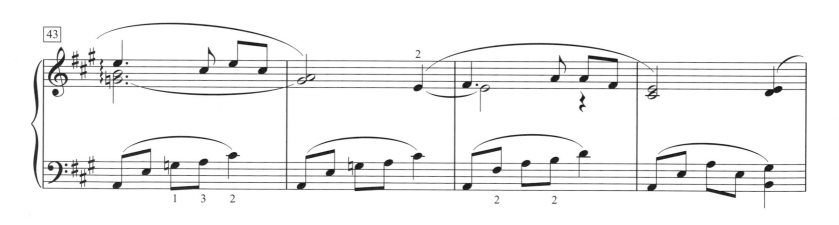

ELEGY

In memory of John Metz

EUGÉNIE ROCHEROLLE

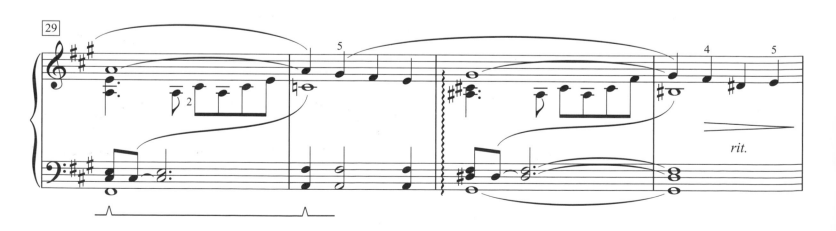

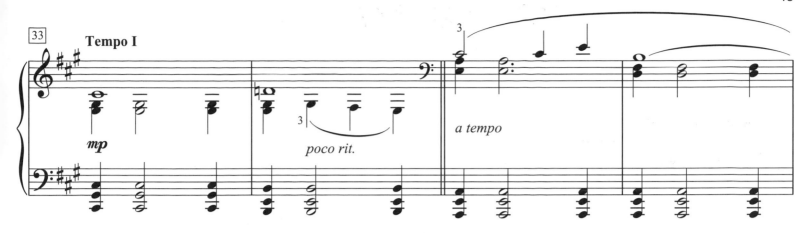

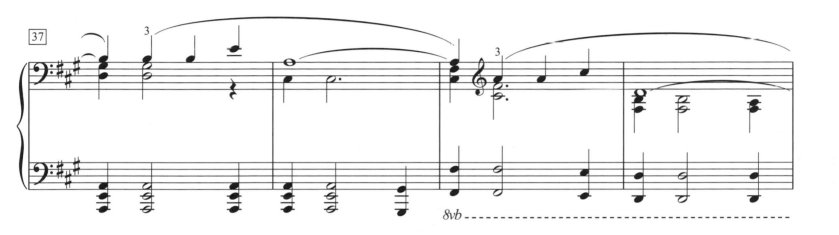

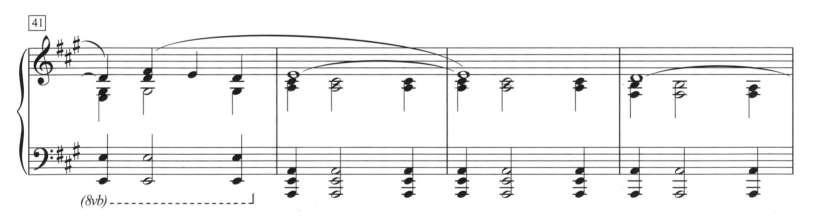

BRIDAL MARCH

for Barbara and Bob MacArthur

Eugénie Rocherolle

RECESSIONAL

EUGÉNIE ROCHEROLLE

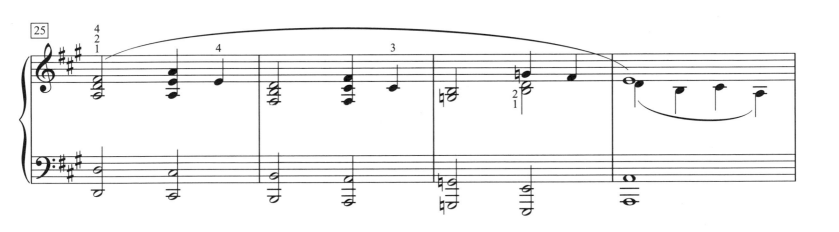

D.C. al Fine

WEDDING MARCH

for Laurent and Holly Rocherolle

EUGÉNIE ROCHEROLLE

WEDDING PROCESSIONAL

Written for Eugénie and Didier's Wedding

EUGÉNIE ROCHEROLLE

* *Ped.*

* *on harmony changes*

THE EUGÉNIE ROCHEROLLE SERIES

Offering both original compositions and popular arrangements, these stunning collections are ideal for intermediate-level pianists! Many include audio tracks performed by Ms. Rocherolle.

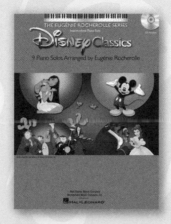

Candlelight Christmas
Eight traditional carols: Away in a Manger • Coventry Carol • Joseph Dearest, Joseph Mine • O Holy Night (duet) • O Little Town of Bethlehem • Silent Night • The Sleep of the Infant Jesus • What Child Is This?
00311808 ....$14.99

Christmas Together
Six piano duet arrangements: Blue Christmas • The Christmas Song (Chestnuts Roasting on an Open Fire) • Rudolph the Red-Nosed Reindeer • Santa Baby • Up on the Housetop • We Wish You a Merry Christmas.
00102838 ....$14.99

Classic Jazz Standards
Ten beloved tunes: Blue Skies • Georgia on My Mind • Isn't It Romantic? • Lazy River • The Nearness of You • On the Sunny Side of the Street • Stardust • Stormy Weather • and more.
00311424 ....$12.99

Continental Suite
Six original piano solos: Belgian Lace • In Old Vienna • La Piazza • Les Avenues De Paris • Oktoberfest • Rondo Capichio.
00312111 ....$12.99

Disney Classics
Nine classic Disney songs: Beauty and the Beast • Bibbidi-Bobbidi-Boo • Chim Chim Cheree • A Dream Is a Wish Your Heart Makes • It's a Small World • Mickey Mouse March • Supercalifragilisticexpialidocious • A Whole New World • Zip-A-Dee-Doo-Dah.
00312272 ....$14.99

Fantasia del Tango
Six original piano solos (and a bonus piano duet!): Bailando Conmigo • Debajo las Estrellas • Ojos de Coqueta • Promesa de Amor • Suenos de Ti • Suspiros • Tango Caprichoso.
00199978 ....$12.99

George Gershwin – Three Preludes
Accessible for intermediate-level pianists: Allegro ben ritmato e deciso • Andante con moto e poco rubato • Agitato.
00111939 ....$10.99

It's Me, O Lord
Nine traditional spirituals: Deep River • It's Me, O Lord • Nobody Knows De Trouble I See • Swing Low, Sweet Chariot • and more.
00311368 ....$12.99

Mancini Classics
Songs: Baby Elephant Walk • Charade • Days of Wine and Roses • Dear Heart • How Soon • Inspector Clouseau Theme • It Had Better Be Tonight • Moment to Moment • Moon River.
00118878 ....$14.99

Meaningful Moments
Eight memorable pieces: Adagio • Bridal March • Elegy • Recessional • Wedding March • Wedding Processional. Plus, arrangements of beloved favorites Amazing Grace and Ave Maria.
00279100 ....$9.99

New Orleans Sketches
Titles: Big Easy Blues • Bourbon Street Beat • Carnival Capers • Jivin' in Jackson Square • Masquerade! • Rex Parade.
00139675..$12.99

On the Jazzy Side
Six original solos. Songs: High Five! • Jubilation! • Prime Time • Small Talk • Small Town Blues • Travelin' Light.
00311982 ....$12.99

Recuerdos Hispanicos
Seven original solos: Brisas Isleñas (Island Breezes) • Dia de Fiesta (Holiday) • Un Amor Quebrado (A Lost Love) • Resonancias de España (Echoes of Spain) • Niña Bonita (Pretty Girl) • Fantasia del Mambo (Mambo Fantasy) • Cuentos del Matador (Tales of the Matador).
00311369 ....$12.99

Rodgers & Hammerstein Selected Favorites
Eight favorites: Climb Ev'ry Mountain • Do-Re-Mi • If I Loved You • Oklahoma • Shall We Dance? • Some Enchanted Evening • There Is Nothin' like a Dame • You'll Never Walk Alone. Includes a CD of Eugénie performing each song.
00311928 ....$14.99

Swingin' the Blues
Six blues originals: Back Street Blues • Big Shot Blues • Easy Walkin' Blues • Hometown Blues • Late Night Blues • Two-Way Blues.
00311445 ....$12.95

Two's Company
Titles: Island Holiday • La Danza • Mood in Blue • Postcript • Whimsical Waltz.
00311883 ....$12.99

Valses Sentimentales
Seven original solos: Bal Masque (Masked Ball) • Jardin de Thé (Tea Garden) • Le Long du Boulevard (Along the Boulevard) • Marché aux Fleurs (Flower Market) • Nuit sans Etoiles (Night Without Stars) • Palais Royale (Royal Palace) • Promenade á Deux (Strolling Together).
00311497 ....$12.95

www.halleonard.com

COMPOSER SHOWCASE
HAL LEONARD STUDENT PIANO LIBRARY

This series showcases great original piano music from our **Hal Leonard Student Piano Library** family of composers, including Bill Boyd, Phillip Keveren, Carol Klose, Jennifer Linn, Mona Rejino, Eugénie Rocherolle and more. Carefully graded for easy selection, each book contains gems that are certain to become classics!

BILL BOYD

JAZZ BITS (AND PIECES)
Early Intermediate Level
00290312 11 Solos.......................$7.99

JAZZ DELIGHTS
Intermediate Level
00240435 11 Solos.......................$7.99

JAZZ FEST
Intermediate Level
00240436 10 Solos.......................$7.99

JAZZ PRELIMS
Early Elementary Level
00290032 12 Solos.......................$6.99

JAZZ SKETCHES
Intermediate Level
00220001 8 Solos.........................$7.99

JAZZ STARTERS
Elementary Level
00290425 10 Solos.......................$6.99

JAZZ STARTERS II
Late Elementary Level
00290434 11 Solos.......................$7.99

JAZZ STARTERS III
Late Elementary Level
00290465 12 Solos.......................$7.99

THINK JAZZ!
Early Intermediate Level
00290417 Method Book..............$10.99

DEBORAH BRADY

PUPPY DOG TALES
Elementary Level
00296718 5 Solos.........................$6.95

TONY CARAMIA

JAZZ MOODS
Intermediate Level
00296728 8 Solos.........................$6.95

SUITE DREAMS
Intermediate Level
00296775 4 Solos.........................$6.99

SONDRA CLARK

DAKOTA DAYS
Intermediate Level
00296521 5 Solos.........................$6.95

FAVORITE CAROLS FOR TWO
Intermediate Level
00296530 5 Duets........................$7.99

FLORIDA FANTASY SUITE
Intermediate Level
00296766 3 Duets........................$7.95

ISLAND DELIGHTS
Intermediate Level
00296666 4 Solos.........................$6.95

THREE ODD METERS
Intermediate Level
00296472 3 Duets........................$6.95

For full descriptions and song lists for the books listed here, and to view a complete list of titles in this series, please visit our website at www.halleonard.com

MATTHEW EDWARDS

CONCERTO FOR YOUNG PIANISTS
FOR 2 PIANOS, FOUR HANDS
Intermediate Level Book/CD
00296356 3 Movements $16.95

CONCERTO NO. 2 IN G MAJOR
FOR 2 PIANOS, 4 HANDS
Intermediate Level Book/CD
00296670 3 Movements...........................$16.95

PHILLIP KEVEREN

MOUSE ON A MIRROR
Late Elementary Level
00296361 5 Solos..................................$6.95

MUSICAL MOODS
Elementary/Late Elementary Level
00296714 7 Solos..................................$5.95

ROMP!
A DIGITAL KEYBOARD ENSEMBLE FOR SIX PLAYERS
Intermediate Level
00296549 Book/CD................................$9.95

SHIFTY-EYED BLUES
Late Elementary Level
00296374 5 Solos..................................$6.99

TEX-MEX REX
Late Elementary Level
00296353 6 Solos..................................$6.99

CAROL KLOSE

CORAL REEF SUITE
Late Elementary Level
00296354 7 Solos..................................$6.99

DESERT SUITE
Intermediate Level
00296667 6 Solos..................................$7.99

FANCIFUL WALTZES
Early Intermediate Level
00296473 5 Solos..................................$7.95

GARDEN TREASURES
Late Intermediate Level
00296787 5 Solos..................................$7.99

ROMANTIC EXPRESSIONS
Intermediate/Late Intermediate Level
00296923 5 Solos..................................$8.99

WATERCOLOR MINIATURES
Early Intermediate Level
00296848 7 Solos..................................$7.99

JENNIFER LINN

AMERICAN IMPRESSIONS
Intermediate Level
00296471 6 Solos..................................$7.99

CHRISTMAS IMPRESSIONS
Intermediate Level
00296706 8 Solos..................................$6.99

JUST PINK
Elementary Level
00296722 9 Solos..................................$6.99

LES PETITES IMAGES
Late Elementary Level
00296664 7 Solos..................................$7.99

LES PETITES IMPRESSIONS
Intermediate Level
00296355 6 Solos..................................$7.99

REFLECTIONS
Late Intermediate Level
00296843 5 Solos..................................$7.99

TALES OF MYSTERY
Intermediate Level
00296769 6 Solos..................................$7.99

MONA REJINO

CIRCUS SUITE
Late Elementary Level
00296665 5 Solos.........................$5.95

JUST FOR KIDS
Elementary Level
00296840 8 Solos.........................$7.99

MERRY CHRISTMAS MEDLEYS
Intermediate Level
00296799 5 Solos.........................$7.99

PORTRAITS IN STYLE
Early Intermediate Level
00296507 6 Solos.........................$7.99

EUGÉNIE ROCHEROLLE

**ENCANTOS ESPAÑOLES
(SPANISH DELIGHTS)**
Intermediate Level
00125451 6 Solos.........................$7.99

JAMBALAYA
FOR 2 PIANOS, 8 HANDS
Intermediate Level
00296654 Piano Ensemble.............$9.99

JAMBALAYA
FOR 2 PIANOS, 4 HANDS
Intermediate Level
00296725 Piano Duo (2 Pianos) $7.95

TOUR FOR TWO
Late Elementary Level
00296832 6 Duets.......................$7.99

TREASURES
Late Elementary/Early Intermediate Level
00296924 7 Solos.........................$8.99

CHRISTOS TSITSAROS

DANCES FROM AROUND THE WORLD
Early Intermediate Level
00296688 7 Solos.........................$6.95

LYRIC BALLADS
Intermediate/Late Intermediate Level
00102404 6 Solos.........................$8.99

POETIC MOMENTS
Intermediate Level
00296403 8 Solos.........................$8.99

SONATINA HUMORESQUE
Late Intermediate Level
00296772 3 Movements $6.99

SONGS WITHOUT WORDS
Intermediate Level
00296506 9 Solos.........................$7.95

THROUGHOUT THE YEAR
Late Elementary Level
00296723 12 Duets......................$6.95

ADDITIONAL COLLECTIONS

ALASKA SKETCHES
by Lynda Lybeck-Robinson
Early Intermediate Level
00119637 8 Solos.........................$7.99

AMERICAN PORTRAITS
by Wendy Stevens
Intermediate Level
00296817 6 Solos.........................$7.99

AT THE LAKE
by Elvina Pearce
Elementary/Late Elementary Level
00131642 10 Solos and Duets.....................$7.99

COUNTY RAGTIME FESTIVAL
by Fred Kern
Intermediate Level
00296882 7 Rags.........................$7.99

PLAY THE BLUES!
by Luann Carman (Method Book)
Early Intermediate Level
00296357 10 Solos.......................$9.99

HAL•LEONARD®
CORPORATION

7777 W. BLUEMOUND RD. P.O. BOX 13819 MILWAUKEE. WI 53213

0814